ROOTS & REFLECTIONS

FAMILY LEGACY JOURNAL

HANDMADE LEATHER EDITION NOW AVAILABLE!

WWW.ROOTSANDREFLECTIONSJOURNAL.COM

10x7 Handmade leather cover, handmade cotton pages with deckled edges. Perfect for gifting and family heirlooms.

reunions

Customize with your family's photos
on orders of five or more

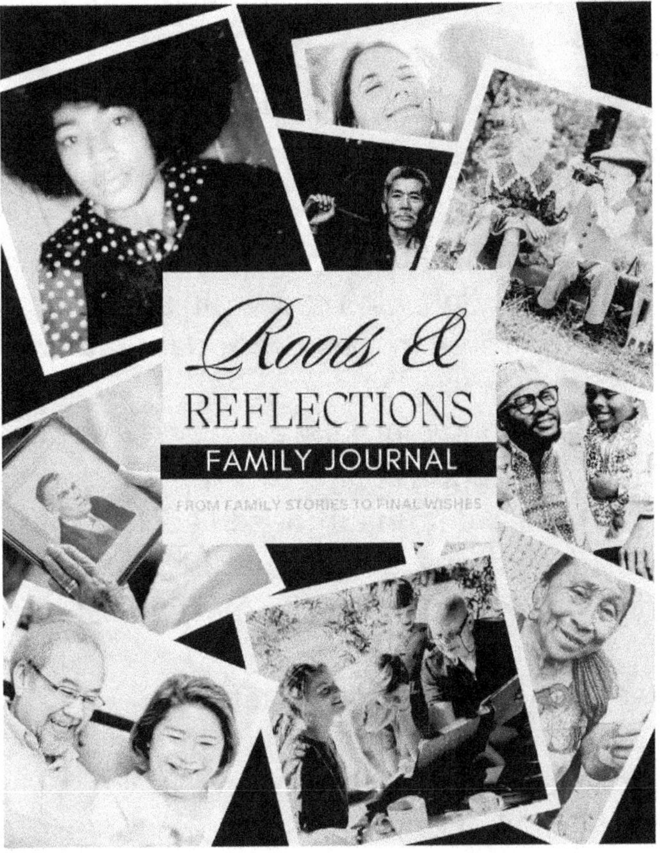

Tailor your book with your family's photos. Only available on orders of 5 or more.

www.rootsandreflectionsjournal.com

DISCLAIMER
Safeguarding Your Family's Legacy

Thank you for choosing Roots & Reflections Family Journal to capture and preserve your family's unique story. Before embarking on this journey of remembrance, please take a moment to read and understand the following disclaimer:

- Sensitive Information:
    - Roots & Reflections Journal is designed to help you document and cherish your family's memories, which may include sensitive and personal information.
    - Exercise caution when recording such details and ensure that the journal is stored in a secure and private location.

- Safeguarding Your Journal:
    - It is your responsibility to keep the journal in a safe and secure place to prevent unauthorized access, loss, or theft.
    - Consider storing the journal in a location known only to you or utilizing additional security measures if necessary.

- Not Responsible for Loss or Theft:
    - Roots & Reflections and its affiliates are not responsible for any damages resulting from the loss or theft of your journal.
    - We recommend taking appropriate precautions to protect the confidentiality and security of the information contained within the journal.

- Acceptance of Terms:
  - The use of Roots & Reflections Journal implies your acceptance of these terms and conditions.
  - By documenting your family's memories in this journal, you acknowledge that you are solely responsible for safeguarding its contents.

- Privacy and Security:
  - While we strive to provide a secure and high-quality product, we cannot guarantee the security of physical items. It is advised to keep sensitive information limited and use discretion in your journaling.

Remember, Roots & Reflections Journal is a treasured keepsake meant to celebrate and preserve your family's legacy. We appreciate your understanding and commitment to ensuring the privacy and security of your family's stories.

Thank you for choosing Roots & Reflections to be a part of your family's journey.

Genuinely,
The Roots & Reflections Team

This journal is dedicated to my mother,
Norva Davenport.

With heartfelt gratitude to my sister,
LaShunda Thomas, for her love,
encouragement, and unwavering support.

TABLE OF CONTENTS

FROM THE AUTHOR

It was a somber day at my favorite uncle's funeral, a day that would ignite the spark for what would become Roots & Reflections. As I sat there, surrounded by grieving family members, something profound unfolded. Stories, laughter, and tears intertwined as various relatives rose to share cherished memories of my uncle, unveiling facets of his life that were, until then, unknown to me. Among these tales were echoes of my late mother, anecdotes that had never reached my ears. I felt the weight of the untold stories, lost forever with those who had left us. We had already lost so many.

In the aftermath of that emotional day, I found myself yearning for a way to capture and preserve the essence of our family's journey. Previous attempts to get everyone together decades earlier to build closer bonds soon fizzled out. The desire still burned within me. Remembering previous youthful attempts to write my own life's journey in empty notebooks long lost, I was determined to not let another family member pass and take such a rich tapestry with them. Lost forever.

Armed with a blank journal, I approached my elder uncle, a repository of family history. I implored him to share stories, memories, and family anecdotes—precious fragments that held keys to our lineage. I especially wanted to know more about my late mother.

This journal wasn't just paper and ink to me; it would be a vessel to encapsulate the wisdom, the laughter, and the legacy of our family. Stories untold of vibrant lives lived and lessons learned. Keys to who they were, and how they came to be who they are.

Days turned into weeks, and weeks into months, but the journal remained blank. Concern welled within me until my uncle finally admitted, "I don't know where to start."

It was in that moment of vulnerability that the seeds of Roots & Reflections were planted. Thinking about the recent loss of my own father and the challenges of navigating through the aftermath without the guidance of information and essential documents.

The stories coming out of a great man that I never really knew the true depth of outside of scratching out a living. A man who also loved preserving family moments from behind the lens of a camcorder. I didn't want another generation to slip away unheard. Unseen. Taking valuable history with them.

Roots & Reflections was born out of love, loss, and the unwavering belief that every family story deserves to be known. Fueled by the desire to provide families with more than just a product—but tools that empower you to preserve, celebrate, and pass down the beauty of your unique narrative and build a legacy.

My commitment is deeply rooted in the understanding that memories, once shared, become timeless treasures. Join me on this journey of remembrance and connection, where every memory tells a story—a story that weaves the tapestry of generations that deserve to be remembered.

Thank you for sharing and being a part of living history. Let's begin our adventure through time, cherishing the past, embracing the present, and building a legacy for the future.

With love and grateful anticipation,

Tameka S. Riley

INTRODUCTION

Welcome to Roots & Reflections, a family journal designed to capture the essence of your unique story, one memory at a time. This journal is not just a collection of blank pages; it's a gateway to explore and celebrate the tapestry of your life, weaving together the threads of your past, present, and hopes for the future.

Purpose and Vision:
The purpose of this journal is to embark on a profound journey through time, gathering the precious moments, stories, and experiences that define your life and family. It's a testament to your history, as well as a bridge to connect generations. With each entry, you preserve your legacy, ensuring that your family's memories remain alive and vibrant for generations to come.

WHY KEEP A FAMILY JOURNAL

A family journal is a vessel for preserving the intangible treasures of our lives. It captures not just facts and figures, but the emotions, values, and wisdom passed down from one generation to the next. This journal invites you to explore and record:

- **Childhood:** The laughter, the tears, the first steps, the discoveries, and the dreams of your early years.

- **Family Life:** The traditions, values, and the stories that make your family unique.

- **Teenage Years:** The moments of transformation, the friendships, the dreams that took root in your youth.

- **Young Adulthood:** The aspirations, the challenges, and the paths chosen as you stepped into the wider world.

- **Adulthood:** The joy, the struggles, and the invaluable lessons learned while raising the next generation. The triumphs, the setbacks, the lessons, and the aspirations you hold for the future.

- **Final Wishes:** In this section, you are free to share information about your vital records, final wishes, and end of life care with your family.

The Power of Storytelling:

This family journal encourages storytelling because it is through storytelling that we transmit the essence of our lives. We pass down not only facts but the deeper understanding of who we are and where we come from. Your stories, insights, and experiences are the bricks that will build a living monument to your family's history.

How To Use This Journal:

This journal contains carefully selected questions to guide you as you document your life story. Whether you write, sketch, or incorporate photos, the pages of this journal are yours to fill as you see fit. There is no right or wrong way to use it. Let your creativity flow, and feel free to share as much or as little as you wish. Insert keepsakes, photos and notes as you go along.

Your Journey Begins:

As we embark on this journey, remember that every word, every memory, and every reflection becomes a legacy. We encourage you to explore these pages with curiosity and an open heart, discovering the richness of our family's story, one entry at a time.

A CALL TO REFLECTION

This journal is a space for you to explore the depths of your memories and experiences. These pages are the canvas upon which your story will unfold. To fully embrace this journey, consider the following guidance:

1. **Create a Safe Space:** This journal is a safe haven for your thoughts and emotions. It's a judgment-free zone where you are free to express your true self.
2. **Embrace Vulnerability:** Embrace the vulnerability of sharing your stories. Sometimes, it's the most candid moments that hold the most profound truths.
3. **Allow Room for Discovery:** As you traverse through the journal sections, remember that you might unearth forgotten memories or gain fresh perspectives on past experiences.
4. **Reflections on Life's Lessons:** Use these pages as a catalyst for introspection. Delve into life's lessons, no matter how significant or seemingly insignificant they might appear.
5. **Embrace Imperfection:** There's no 'right' way to document your story. Embrace imperfections as part of the beauty in telling your story.

TIPS FOR ENGAGING WITH THIS JOURNAL:

- **Take your time:** Reflecting on your life journey is a process, not a race. Allow yourself the time needed to explore and articulate your thoughts and memories.
- **Regular engagement:** Make it a habit to revisit the journal regularly. The act of chronicling your story is as valuable as the story itself.
- **Share Keepsakes:** Feel free to slip photos, notes and keepsakes between the pages for your loved ones.
- **Share and discuss:** Consider sharing your reflections with family members. Each entry may spark further conversations and bring deeper understanding.

LEAVE YOUR MARK

This journal is a tapestry waiting to be woven, and you are the weaver of its intricate threads. It's an opportunity to embrace the unique narrative of your family, to celebrate the highs and lows, and to share the wisdom gained along the way.

Turn the page and step into the first section that resonates with you. Allow your story to unfold, capturing the essence of who you are and how your journey intertwines across generations.

"THERE IS NO GREATER
AGONY THAN BEARING AN
UNTOLD STORY INSIDE OF
YOU."
-MAYA ANGELOU

ROOTS & REFLECTIONS

FAMILY LEGACY JOURNAL

THE TAPESTRY OF MY LIFE AS TOLD BY

____

Name

IN MY OWN WORDS

Chapter 1

Childhood Memories

Secret Hideaways and Sweet Whispers:
A Window into Childhood

Share names, birthdays & origins

Mother

____

Father

____

Grandparents (Mother's Side)

____

____

Grandparents (Father's Side)

____

____

Great Grandparents

____

____

____

Before I formed you in the womb I knew you, before you were born I set you apart –
Jeremiah 1:5

When and where were you born?

____

____

____

____

Are you the youngest, middle or oldest child?

____

____

What nicknames did you have?

____

____

____

____

Before I formed you in the womb I knew you, before you were born I set you apart –
Jeremiah 1:5

What is your family tree as you know it?

Before I formed you in the womb I knew you, before you were born I set you apart –
Jeremiah 1:5

Continue your family tree or add photos to this space.

Before I formed you in the womb I knew you, before you were born I set you apart -
Jeremiah 1:5

What is your earliest childhood memory?

____

____

____

____

____

____

____

____

____

____

Before I formed you in the womb I knew you, before you were born I set you apart –
Jeremiah 1:5

Did you have any favorite bedtime stories or lullabies?

____

____

____

____

What were your favorite toys or games?

____

____

____

____

____

____

Before I formed you in the womb I knew you, before you were born I set you apart –
Jeremiah 1:5

Your Firsts

First Word

____

First Steps

____

First Day of School

____

Photographs

Before I formed you in the womb I knew you, before you were born I set you apart –
Jeremiah 1:5

Your Firsts

First Pet

____

____

First Friend

____

____

First Crush

____

____

Photographs

Before I formed you in the womb I knew you, before you were born I set you apart –
Jeremiah 1:5

What elementary school did you attend?

Who was your favorite teacher?

What were your favorite subjects & activities?

Before I formed you in the womb I knew you, before you were born I set you apart –
Jeremiah 1:5

Describe a typical day after school.

____

____

____

____

Who were some of your neighborhood friends?

____

____

____

____

____

Before I formed you in the womb I knew you, before you were born I set you apart –
Jeremiah 1:5

What was your favorite hiding place or secret spot?

____

____

____

What did you want to be when you grew up?

____

____

____

What was your inspiration or motivation?

____

____

____

____

Before I formed you in the womb I knew you, before you were born I set you apart –
Jeremiah 1:5

Did you have a favorite aunt, uncle or grandparent?

____

____

____

____

What was your favorite meal for mom to make?

____

____

____

____

____

Before I formed you in the womb I knew you, before you were born I set you apart –
Jeremiah 1:5

What home remedies made you cringe?

Before I formed you in the womb I knew you, before you were born I set you apart –
Jeremiah 1:5

Did any of the home remedies work?

Before I formed you in the womb I knew you, before you were born I set you apart –
Jeremiah 1:5

Did you have any other pets?

____

____

____

____

What was your worst punishment as a child? Why were you punished?

____

____

____

____

____

Before I formed you in the womb I knew you, before you were born I set you apart –
Jeremiah 1:5

Share a funny or embarrassing childhood story.

Before I formed you in the womb I knew you, before you were born I set you apart –
Jeremiah 1:5

Photographs

Before I formed you in the womb I knew you, before you were born I set you apart –
Jeremiah 1:5

Share childhood fears or challenges you overcame?

____

____

____

____

____

____

____

____

____

Before I formed you in the womb I knew you, before you were born I set you apart -
Jeremiah 1:5

Share a moment you are particularly proud of.

Before I formed you in the womb I knew you, before you were born I set you apart –
Jeremiah 1:5

What was your favorite thing to do with your mom?

____

____

____

____

What was your favorite thing to do with your dad?

____

____

____

____

Before I formed you in the womb I knew you, before you were born I set you apart –
Jeremiah 1:5

What were some of your favorite songs?

____

____

____

____

____

Favorite dances?

____

____

____

____

____

Before I formed you in the womb I knew you, before you were born I set you apart –
Jeremiah 1:5

What were some of your favorite shows or movies?

____

____

____

____

What were some of your hobbies?

____

____

____

____

____

Before I formed you in the womb I knew you, before you were born I set you apart –
Jeremiah 1:5

What were some key family values instilled in you?

____

____

____

____

What is something you wish your parents knew?

____

____

____

____

____

Before I formed you in the womb I knew you, before you were born I set you apart –
Jeremiah 1:5

What are some things you are thankful for?

____

____

____

____

____

____

____

____

____

Before I formed you in the womb I knew you, before you were born I set you apart –
Jeremiah 1:5

Chapter 2

Family Life

Heartbeats of Home:
The Tapestry of Our Family

How did your parents meet?

____

____

____

____

____

What did your parents do for a living?

____

____

____

____

____

Before I formed you in the womb I knew you, before you were born I set you apart –
Jeremiah 1:5

Describe the dynamic between your parents?

____

____

____

____

____

Where was your family living during this time?

____

____

____

____

____

Before I formed you in the womb I knew you, before you were born I set you apart –
Jeremiah 1:5

List your sibling, birthdays, nicknames, etc.

Before I formed you in the womb I knew you, before you were born I set you apart –
Jeremiah 1:5

Share some of your favorite holiday memories.

____

____

____

____

____

____

____

____

____

____

Before I formed you in the womb I knew you, before you were born I set you apart –
Jeremiah 1:5

Photographs

Before I formed you in the womb I knew you, before you were born I set you apart –
Jeremiah 1:5

Share a memory about trips or vacations taken.

____

____

____

____

____

____

____

____

____

____

Before I formed you in the womb I knew you, before you were born I set you apart –
Jeremiah 1:5

Photographs

Before I formed you in the womb I knew you, before you were born I set you apart –
Jeremiah 1:5

What traditions stand out to you?

Before I formed you in the womb I knew you, before you were born I set you apart –
Jeremiah 1:5

What traditions do you still observe today?

Before I formed you in the womb I knew you, before you were born I set you apart –
Jeremiah 1:5

What hardships did your family overcome & how?

____

____

____

____

____

____

____

____

____

____

Before I formed you in the womb I knew you, before you were born I set you apart –
Jeremiah 1:5

Share any family anecdotes or stories passed down through the family.

____

____

____

____

____

____

____

____

____

Before I formed you in the womb I knew you, before you were born I set you apart –
Jeremiah 1:5

Describe your childhood home.

Before I formed you in the womb I knew you, before you were born I set you apart –
Jeremiah 1:5

Describe your childhood neighborhood, neighbors & friends.

____

____

____

____

____

____

____

____

____

____

Before I formed you in the womb I knew you, before you were born I set you apart –
Jeremiah 1:5

Were there any family recipes or dishes that hold special meaning to you?

____

____

____

____

____

____

____

____

____

Before I formed you in the womb I knew you, before you were born I set you apart –
Jeremiah 1:5

Were there any exceptional individuals who played a significant role in your family?

____

____

____

____

____

____

____

____

Before I formed you in the womb I knew you, before you were born I set you apart –
Jeremiah 1:5

Share instances of family members showing exceptional courage, kindness, or resilience.

Before I formed you in the womb I knew you, before you were born I set you apart –
Jeremiah 1:5

What were the most profound lessons or words of wisdom passed down to you?

____

____

____

____

____

____

____

____

Before I formed you in the womb I knew you, before you were born I set you apart –
Jeremiah 1:5

Photographs

Before I formed you in the womb I knew you, before you were born I set you apart –
Jeremiah 1:5

Chapter 3

Teenage Years

Unraveling Adolescence:
Journeys of Discovery & Adventure

Describe your teenage years.

Before I formed you in the womb I knew you, before you were born I set you apart –
Jeremiah 1:5

What Jr. High School Did You Attend?

____

____

Who were your favorite teachers & why

____

____

____

____

____

____

Before I formed you in the womb I knew you, before you were born I set you apart –
Jeremiah 1:5

Who were some of your closest friends in Jr. High?

____

____

____

____

Did you have a part-time job?

____

____

____

____

____

Before I formed you in the womb I knew you, before you were born I set you apart –
Jeremiah 1:5

Photographs

Before I formed you in the womb I knew you, before you were born I set you apart –
Jeremiah 1:5

Share sports or extra curricular activities.

Photographs

Before I formed you in the womb I knew you, before you were born I set you apart –
Jeremiah 1:5

Share Your Firsts

Teenage Crush

____

First Job

____

First Driving Experience

____

____

____

____

____

Before I formed you in the womb I knew you, before you were born I set you apart –
Jeremiah 1:5

More Firsts

First Concert

____

____

____

First Love

____

First Time Saving For A Major Purchase

____

____

____

____

____

____

Before I formed you in the womb I knew you, before you were born I set you apart –
Jeremiah 1:5

What High School Did You Attend?

____

____

Who were your favorite teachers & why

____

____

____

____

____

____

____

Before I formed you in the womb I knew you, before you were born I set you apart –
Jeremiah 1:5

Who were some of your friends in High School?

____

____

____

____

Did you have a part-time job?

____

____

____

____

____

Before I formed you in the womb I knew you, before you were born I set you apart –
Jeremiah 1:5

Photographs

Before I formed you in the womb I knew you, before you were born I set you apart –
Jeremiah 1:5

What crowd did you hang out with?

____

____

____

____

Did you play sports or belong to any organizations?

____

____

____

____

____

Before I formed you in the womb I knew you, before you were born I set you apart –
Jeremiah 1:5

How did your relationship with your parents change?

____

____

____

____

____

What were their hopes & dreams for you?

____

____

____

____

Before I formed you in the womb I knew you, before you were born I set you apart -
Jeremiah 1:5

What were your own dreams and aspirations?

____

____

____

____

Did you have any hobbies?

____

____

____

____

____

____

____

Before I formed you in the womb I knew you, before you were born I set you apart –
Jeremiah 1:5

Who were your role models?

____

____

____

____

How did you navigate peer pressure & challenges?

____

____

____

____

____

____

Before I formed you in the womb I knew you, before you were born I set you apart –
Jeremiah 1:5

What were your favorite hair styles & fashions?

Photographs

Before I formed you in the womb I knew you, before you were born I set you apart –
Jeremiah 1:5

Who was the 'teenage heartthrob' during that time?

____

____

____

Did you ever meet anyone famous?

____

____

____

____

____

____

____

Before I formed you in the womb I knew you, before you were born I set you apart –
Jeremiah 1:5

Share about your prom.

Photographs

Before I formed you in the womb I knew you, before you were born I set you apart –
Jeremiah 1:5

Where were your favorite places to hang out?

What things or causes were you passionate about?

Before I formed you in the womb I knew you, before you were born I set you apart –
Jeremiah 1:5

Were there any books, movies, or music that had a profound impact on your worldview?

____

____

____

____

Share a moment you would describe as your "15 minutes of fame".

____

____

____

____

____

Before I formed you in the womb I knew you, before you were born I set you apart –
Jeremiah 1:5

What were some things you got away with that you never told your parents?

____

____

____

____

____

____

____

____

____

Before I formed you in the womb I knew you, before you were born I set you apart –
Jeremiah 1:5

Before I formed you in the womb I knew you, before you were born I set you apart –
Jeremiah 1:5

What was the biggest trouble you got into?

Before I formed you in the womb I knew you, before you were born I set you apart –
Jeremiah 1:5

Were there any deeply personal or emotional struggles you had to overcome? How did you do it?

____

____

____

____

____

____

____

____

____

____

Before I formed you in the womb I knew you, before you were born I set you apart –
Jeremiah 1:5

Before I formed you in the womb I knew you, before you were born I set you apart –
Jeremiah 1:5

Share a funny or embarrassing moment.

Before I formed you in the womb I knew you, before you were born I set you apart –
Jeremiah 1:5

How did you envision your future as a young adult?

____

____

____

____

____

____

____

____

____

____

Before I formed you in the womb I knew you, before you were born I set you apart –
Jeremiah 1:5

Photographs

Before I formed you in the womb I knew you, before you were born I set you apart –
Jeremiah 1:5

Share a moment you were particularly proud of.

Before I formed you in the womb I knew you, before you were born I set you apart –
Jeremiah 1:5

If you could give your teenage self advice, what would it be?

____

____

____

____

____

____

____

____

____

Before I formed you in the womb I knew you, before you were born I set you apart –
Jeremiah 1:5

What would you do if you knew you couldn't fail?

____

____

____

____

____

____

When do you plan to begin?

____

____

____

____

____

Before I formed you in the womb I knew you, before you were born I set you apart –
Jeremiah 1:5

Chapter 4

Young Adult

Unfolding Horizons:
Journeys Beyond Boundaries

Describe your years as a young adult.

Before I formed you in the womb I knew you, before you were born I set you apart –
Jeremiah 1:5

Share about your time at college.

Before I formed you in the womb I knew you, before you were born I set you apart –
Jeremiah 1:5

Photographs

Before I formed you in the womb I knew you, before you were born I set you apart –
Jeremiah 1:5

Who or what influenced your career path?

Before I formed you in the womb I knew you, before you were born I set you apart -
Jeremiah 1:5

Your Firsts

First Taste of Independence

____

____

____

____

First House or Apartment

____

____

____

First Professional Job

____

____

____

____

Before I formed you in the womb I knew you, before you were born I set you apart –
Jeremiah 1:5

Share some of your 'firsts'.

First Significant Travel Experience

____

____

____

First Major Life Decision

____

____

____

First Serious Relationship

____

____

____

____

____

Before I formed you in the womb I knew you, before you were born I set you apart –
Jeremiah 1:5

Photographs

Before I formed you in the womb I knew you, before you were born I set you apart –
Jeremiah 1:5

Share some major turning points or crossroads.

____

____

____

____

____

____

____

____

____

____

Before I formed you in the womb I knew you, before you were born I set you apart -
Jeremiah 1:5

Share some major life challenges or adversities, and how you overcame them.

____

____

____

____

____

____

____

____

____

Before I formed you in the womb I knew you, before you were born I set you apart –
Jeremiah 1:5

Before I formed you in the womb I knew you, before you were born I set you apart
- Jeremiah 1:5

Were there any personal or professional achievements that hold special meaning for you?

____

____

____

____

____

____

____

____

____

____

Before I formed you in the womb I knew you, before you were born I set you apart –
Jeremiah 1:5

Before I formed you in the womb I knew you, before you were born I set you apart –
Jeremiah 1:5

How did you meet your significant other?

____

____

____

____

____

Photographs

Before I formed you in the womb I knew you, before you were born I set you apart –
Jeremiah 1:5

When did you know they were the one?

Describe your first date.

Before I formed you in the womb I knew you, before you were born I set you apart –
Jeremiah 1:5

Describe the proposal.

____

____

____

____

____

____

Photographs

Before I formed you in the womb I knew you, before you were born I set you apart –
Jeremiah 1:5

Describe your wedding day.

____

____

____

____

____

____

____

____

____

____

Before I formed you in the womb I knew you, before you were born I set you apart –
Jeremiah 1:5

What challenges and objections did you overcome?

Before I formed you in the womb I knew you, before you were born I set you apart –
Jeremiah 1:5

Photographs

Before I formed you in the womb I knew you, before you were born I set you apart –
Jeremiah 1:5

Discuss some of your innermost hopes & dreams?

____

____

____

____

Share your innermost hopes & dreams for your children.

____

____

____

____

____

Before I formed you in the womb I knew you, before you were born I set you apart –
Jeremiah 1:5

What things were you passionate about?

____

____

____

____

Describe where you were living during this time.

____

____

____

____

____

____

Before I formed you in the womb I knew you, before you were born I set you apart –
Jeremiah 1:5

Share experiences of mentorship or guidance from someone who played a vital role in your life.

____

____

____

____

____

____

____

____

____

____

Before I formed you in the womb I knew you, before you were born I set you apart –
Jeremiah 1:5

Describe a moment of self discovery when you knew you were officially 'adulting'.

Before I formed you in the womb I knew you, before you were born I set you apart –
Jeremiah 1:5

Photographs

Before I formed you in the womb I knew you, before you were born I set you apart –
Jeremiah 1:5

If you could give your young adult self a piece of advice, what would it be?

____

____

____

____

____

____

____

____

____

Before I formed you in the womb I knew you, before you were born I set you apart –
Jeremiah 1:5

Chapter 5

Adulthood

Chronicles of Adulthood:
Navigating Life's Peaks and Valleys

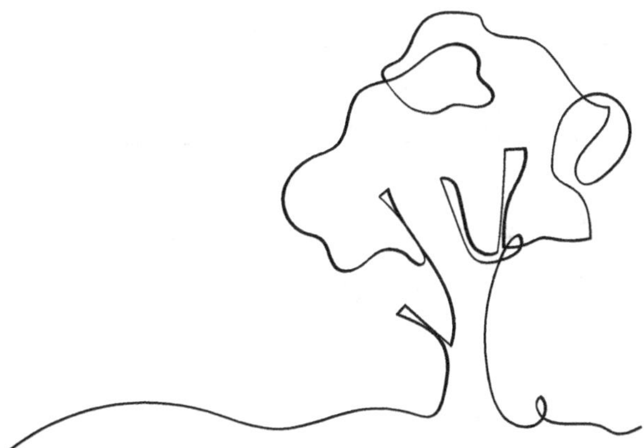

How would you describe your adult years?

Before I formed you in the womb I knew you, before you were born I set you apart –
Jeremiah 1:5

How many states have you lived in and where?

____

____

____

____

____

____

____

____

____

____

Before I formed you in the womb I knew you, before you were born I set you apart –
Jeremiah 1:5

When did you purchase your first home? Where was it? What drew you to it?

Before I formed you in the womb I knew you, before you were born I set you apart -
Jeremiah 1:5

Photographs

Before I formed you in the womb I knew you, before you were born I set you apart –
Jeremiah 1:5

How many children do you have? Share their names (include nicknames). What are their birthdays?

Before I formed you in the womb I knew you, before you were born I set you apart –
Jeremiah 1:5

Describe the moment you learned that you were going to be a parent for the first time.

____

____

____

____

____

____

____

____

____

____

Before I formed you in the womb I knew you, before you were born I set you apart –
Jeremiah 1:5

Photographs

Before I formed you in the womb I knew you, before you were born I set you apart –
Jeremiah 1:5

First Child

What was your due date? ___________________________

When Did You Find Out? ___________________________

Where were you? What was your reaction?

____

____

How did you tell the family?

____

____

____

What was their reaction?

____

____

____

Before I formed you in the womb I knew you, before you were born I set you apart –
Jeremiah 1:5

How did you choose your first child's name?

____

____

____

____

____

What were some other names you considered?

____

____

____

____

____

Before I formed you in the womb I knew you, before you were born I set you apart –
Jeremiah 1:5

Photographs

Before I formed you in the womb I knew you, before you were born I set you apart –
Jeremiah 1:5

Second Child

What was your due date? ___________________________

When Did You Find Out? ___________________________

Where were you? What was your reaction?

____

____

How did you tell the family?

____

____

____

What was their reaction?

____

____

____

____

Before I formed you in the womb I knew you, before you were born I set you apart –
Jeremiah 1:5

How did you choose your second child's name?

____

____

____

____

What were some other names you considered?

____

____

____

____

Before I formed you in the womb I knew you, before you were born I set you apart –
Jeremiah 1:5

Photographs

Before I formed you in the womb I knew you, before you were born I set you apart –
Jeremiah 1:5

Third Child

What was your due date? ______________________________

When Did You Find Out? ______________________________

Where were you? What was your reaction?

____

____

How did you tell the family?

____

____

What was their reaction?

____

____

____

Before I formed you in the womb I knew you, before you were born I set you apart –
Jeremiah 1:5

How did you choose your third child's name?

____

____

____

____

____

What were some other names you considered?

____

____

____

____

Before I formed you in the womb I knew you, before you were born I set you apart -
Jeremiah 1:5

Photographs

Before I formed you in the womb I knew you, before you were born I set you apart –
Jeremiah 1:5

Fourth Child

What was your due date?

When Did You Find Out?

Where were you? What was your reaction?

____

____

How did you tell the family?

____

____

What was their reaction?

____

____

____

Before I formed you in the womb I knew you, before you were born I set you apart –
Jeremiah 1:5

How did you choose your fourth child's name?

____

____

____

____

____

What were some other names you considered?

____

____

____

____

____

____

Before I formed you in the womb I knew you, before you were born I set you apart –
Jeremiah 1:5

Before I formed you in the womb I knew you, before you were born I set you apart -
Jeremiah 1:5

Photographs

Before I formed you in the womb I knew you, before you were born I set you apart –
Jeremiah 1:5

How has your parenting style evolved over the years?

____

____

____

____

____

____

____

____

____

Before I formed you in the womb I knew you, before you were born I set you apart -
Jeremiah 1:5

____

____

____

____

____

____

____

____

____

____

Before I formed you in the womb I knew you, before you were born I set you apart –
Jeremiah 1:5

What were the most memorable moments with each child?

____

____

____

____

____

____

____

____

____

____

Before I formed you in the womb I knew you, before you were born I set you apart –
Jeremiah 1:5

Before I formed you in the womb I knew you, before you were born I set you apart –
Jeremiah 1:5

Before I formed you in the womb I knew you, before you were born I set you apart –
Jeremiah 1:5

Before I formed you in the womb I knew you, before you were born I set you apart –
Jeremiah 1:5

Photographs

Before I formed you in the womb I knew you, before you were born I set you apart –
Jeremiah 1:5

What lessons or values did you aim to pass on to your children?

Before I formed you in the womb I knew you, before you were born I set you apart –
Jeremiah 1:5

What parenting challenges stand out to you?

____

____

____

____

____

____

____

____

____

____

Before I formed you in the womb I knew you, before you were born I set you apart –
Jeremiah 1:5

What moment are you particularly proud of?

____

____

____

____

____

____

____

____

____

Before I formed you in the womb I knew you, before you were born I set you apart –
Jeremiah 1:5

Share some of the most memorable family vacations or activities with your children?

Before I formed you in the womb I knew you, before you were born I set you apart –
Jeremiah 1:5

Photographs

Before I formed you in the womb I knew you, before you were born I set you apart –
Jeremiah 1:5

Did you have any unique ways of bonding with your children?

Before I formed you in the womb I knew you, before you were born I set you apart –
Jeremiah 1:5

Were there any traditions you created as a parent?

Before I formed you in the womb I knew you, before you were born I set you apart –
Jeremiah 1:5

Share some of your parenting highlights & lowlights?

____

____

____

____

____

____

____

____

____

____

____

Before I formed you in the womb I knew you, before you were born I set you apart –
Jeremiah 1:5

Before I formed you in the womb I knew you, before you were born I set you apart –
Jeremiah 1:5

What were some of your biggest fears as a parent?

Before I formed you in the womb I knew you, before you were born I set you apart -
Jeremiah 1:5

What moments of personal growth & transformation have resulted from your experiences as a parent?

____

____

____

____

____

____

____

____

____

Before I formed you in the womb I knew you, before you were born I set you apart –
Jeremiah 1:5

Before I formed you in the womb I knew you, before you were born I set you apart –
Jeremiah 1:5

Photographs

Before I formed you in the womb I knew you, before you were born I set you apart –
Jeremiah 1:5

What are your proudest personal or professional achievements?

____

____

____

____

____

____

____

____

____

____

Before I formed you in the womb I knew you, before you were born I set you apart –
Jeremiah 1:5

Before I formed you in the womb I knew you, before you were born I set you apart –
Jeremiah 1:5

How have your hobbies and interests evolved?

Before I formed you in the womb I knew you, before you were born I set you apart –
Jeremiah 1:5

Describe a time when you were at the top of your game.

____

____

____

____

____

Photograph

Before I formed you in the womb I knew you, before you were born I set you apart –
Jeremiah 1:5

Share some major life-changing experiences or epiphanies?

Before I formed you in the womb I knew you, before you were born I set you apart -
Jeremiah 1:5

Share a moment in your life you wish you handled differently.

____

____

____

____

____

____

____

____

____

Before I formed you in the womb I knew you, before you were born I set you apart –
Jeremiah 1:5

Share personal philosophies & wisdom that has emerged from your life experiences.

Before I formed you in the womb I knew you, before you were born I set you apart –
Jeremiah 1:5

What are your most cherished memories from this time?

____

____

____

____

____

____

____

____

____

Before I formed you in the womb I knew you, before you were born I set you apart –
Jeremiah 1:5

Photographs

Before I formed you in the womb I knew you, before you were born I set you apart –
Jeremiah 1:5

What is something you wish your children knew?

Before I formed you in the womb I knew you, before you were born I set you apart –
Jeremiah 1:5

Before I formed you in the womb I knew you, before you were born I set you apart –
Jeremiah 1:5

What is something you wish your spouse knew?

Before I formed you in the womb I knew you, before you were born I set you apart -
Jeremiah 1:5

Before I formed you in the womb I knew you, before you were born I set you apart –
Jeremiah 1:5

How do you envision the future, and what hopes and dreams do you hold now?

Before I formed you in the womb I knew you, before you were born I set you apart –
Jeremiah 1:5

What's a moment in time you wish you could experience all over again?

____

____

____

____

____

____

____

____

____

____

Before I formed you in the womb I knew you, before you were born I set you apart –
Jeremiah 1:5

Share your bucket list.

____

____

____

____

____

____

____

____

____

Before I formed you in the womb I knew you, before you were born I set you apart –
Jeremiah 1:5

How would you like to be remembered?

____

____

____

____

____

____

____

____

____

____

Before I formed you in the womb I knew you, before you were born I set you apart –
Jeremiah 1:5

What are some thoughts and wishes you would like to share with your loved ones?

Before I formed you in the womb I knew you, before you were born I set you apart –
Jeremiah 1:5

Before I formed you in the womb I knew you, before you were born I set you apart –
Jeremiah 1:5

Before I formed you in the womb I knew you, before you were born I set you apart –
Jeremiah 1:5

Photographs

Before I formed you in the womb I knew you, before you were born I set you apart –
Jeremiah 1:5

Chapter 6

Final Wishes & Vital Information

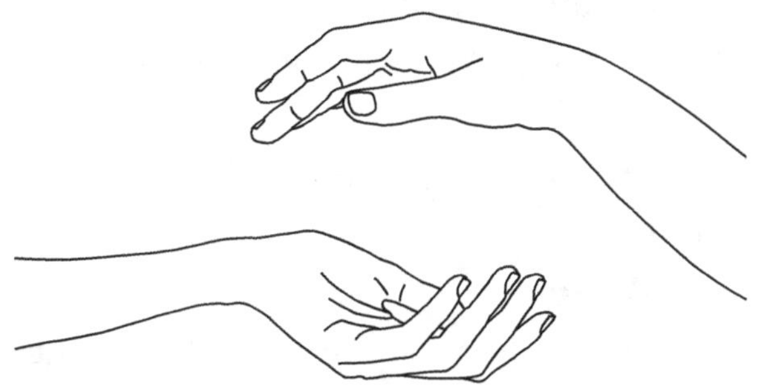

Final Wishes & Vital Information

When reflecting on final wishes, it's important to consider the legacy one wishes to leave behind and the preferences for end-of-life decisions. Here are some questions you might consider answering for your family on the following pages:

1. **Legacy and Remembrance:**
   - How would you like to be remembered?
   - Is there a specific message or piece of wisdom you'd like to pass on to future generations?

2. **Funeral or Memorial Wishes:**
   - Would you like to share any input on your funeral or memorial service?
   - Are there specific songs, readings, or rituals you would like to be included?
   - Have you considered whether you prefer burial or cremation?

3. **Personal Belongings and Distributions:**
   - Have you decided how you would like your personal belongings to be distributed among family or friends?
   - Is there an item or heirloom you would like for someone to have?

4. **Healthcare and End-of-Life Decisions:**
   - Do you have specific wishes regarding end-of-life care and medical decisions?
   - Have you considered whether you would like to create an advance directive or living will?

5. **Financial and Legal Matters:**
   - Have you prepared a will or estate plan? Are there any changes or updates you wish to make?
   - Have you documented your financial accounts, passwords, and important information for your loved ones?
   - Where paperwork and policy information be found?

Final Wishes & Vital Information

6. **Letter or Message:**
   - Would you like to write a final letter or message to your loved ones?

7. **Celebration of Life:**
   - Would you like a celebration or gathering in your honor, rather than a traditional funeral service?
   - How would you like this celebration to be conducted?

8. **Charitable or Donations Preferences:**
   - Are there specific charities or causes you would like to support in your memory?
   - Do you wish for donations to be made to any particular organizations or foundations?

9. **Cultural or Religious Preferences:**
   - Are there cultural or religious customs or ceremonies you wish to be included in your final wishes?
   -

These questions serve as a guide for you to consider and document your final wishes. Discussing these topics with loved ones can be difficult. Use this as a guide to help ensure that your preferences are known and respected when the time comes.

Before I formed you in the womb I knew you, before you were born I set you apart –
Jeremiah 1:5

What final wishes would you like to share with your family? Do you have preferences for your funeral or memorial service?

____

____

____

____

____

____

____

____

____

____

Before I formed you in the womb I knew you, before you were born I set you apart –
Jeremiah 1:5

Before I formed you in the womb I knew you, before you were born I set you apart –
Jeremiah 1:5

Are there specific songs, readings, or rituals you would like to be included?

____

____

____

____

____

____

____

____

____

____

Before I formed you in the womb I knew you, before you were born I set you apart –
Jeremiah 1:5

Have you considered whether you prefer burial or cremation?

____

____

____

Have you named beneficiaries on your bank accounts to avoid probate?

____

____

Use this space to share life insurance policy information with your family.

____

____

____

____

Before I formed you in the womb I knew you, before you were born I set you apart –
Jeremiah 1:5

Medical Insurance Company & Policy #

____

____

Mortgage Company & Account #

____

____

Automobile Finance Company & Account #

____

____

Homeowners Insurance Company & Account #

____

____

____

____

Before I formed you in the womb I knew you, before you were born I set you apart –
Jeremiah 1:5

Do you have any storage units? If so where?

____

____

____

Use this space to share safe deposit boxes, investments, & other information you would like to share with your family.

____

____

____

____

____

____

Before I formed you in the womb I knew you, before you were born I set you apart –
Jeremiah 1:5

Have you decided how you would like your personal belongings handled?

____

____

____

____

____

____

____

____

____

Before I formed you in the womb I knew you, before you were born I set you apart –
Jeremiah 1:5

Is there an item or heirloom you would like to make sure someone receives?

____

____

____

____

____

____

____

____

____

____

Before I formed you in the womb I knew you, before you were born I set you apart –
Jeremiah 1:5

Before I formed you in the womb I knew you, before you were born I set you apart –
Jeremiah 1:5

Do you have specific wishes regarding end-of-life care and medical decisions?

Before I formed you in the womb I knew you, before you were born I set you apart -
Jeremiah 1:5

Have you considered whether you would like to create an advance directive or living will?

____

____

____

Where can your family find important documents and banking information?

____

____

____

____

____

Before I formed you in the womb I knew you, before you were born I set you apart -
Jeremiah 1:5

Have you documented your financial accounts, passwords, and important information for your loved ones?

____

____

____

____

____

____

____

____

Before I formed you in the womb I knew you, before you were born I set you apart –
Jeremiah 1:5

Before I formed you in the womb I knew you, before you were born I set you apart –
Jeremiah 1:5

If you could leave a final message for your loved ones, what would it be?

____

____

____

____

____

____

____

____

____

Before I formed you in the womb I knew you, before you were born I set you apart –
Jeremiah 1:5

Before I formed you in the womb I knew you, before you were born I set you apart –
Jeremiah 1:5

Before I formed you in the womb I knew you, before you were born I set you apart –
Jeremiah 1:5

ROOTS & REFLECTIONS

ISBN: 979-8-218-97064-2
AUTHOR: Tameka S. Riley
PUBLISHER: RileyMedia.us

Handmade leather edition available at **www.rootsandreflectionsjournal.com**